# MACHINE LEARNING

# FOR BEGINNERS

YOUR COMPREHENSIVE GUIDE FOR
MARKOV MODELS, REINFORCE
LEARNING, MODEL EVALUATION, SVM,
NAIVE BAYES CLASSIFIER
(BOOK 3)

By Ken Richards

Author and Researcher

ISBN 13: 978-1983-4340-82
ISBN 10: 1983-4340-86

# MACHINE LEARNING

## FOR BEGINNERS

YOUR COMPREHESIVE
GUIDE FOR MARKOV
MODELS, REINFORCE
LEARNING, MODEL
EVALUATION, SVM,
NAIVES BAYES
CLASSIFIER

**KEN RICHARDS**

# TABLE OF CONTENTS

# PREFACE

This book is a discussion about advanced machine learning. The book is more detailed compared to what was discussed in the first and second machine learning books.

Markov models will be explored in detail, hence, you will know how to use them in machine learning. Reinforcement learning has also been discussed. You will learn the various reinforcement learning algorithms.

Structured prediction, which is one of the advanced machine learning topics, has been explored. The author helps you understand how to use the Naïve Bayes classifier to do machine learning tasks.

The Support Vector Machine is very popular in machine learning. This has been discussed in this book. Once you have trained a machine learning model, it is good for you to evaluate it to know whether it will perform well in a production environment. The author helps you know how to evaluate your trained model by evaluating several parameters.

Machine learning is applied in various fields. The various applications of machine learning in the various sectors has been discussed. You will know how machine learning is applied in sectors such as banking, transport, logistics, etc.

Recommender systems have also been explored. You may need to study a course related to machine learning. There are various institutions that offer degree programs in machine related courses. These institutions have been discussed. They have been categorized into those that offer full-time programs and those that offer part-time programs. The future of machine learning has also been discussed.

# Chapter 1

# Introduction

Human beings can learn from experience. Human beings show an improvement from time to time when reacting to the same experience. When teaching yourself how to play a game, you will show an improvement every time you play.

Machine learning involves the design and development of computer systems capable of showing an improvement with time. The improvement usually results from experience. The concept of machine learning was borrowed from the learning behavior of human beings. Research has shown that just like human beings, computers are able to show an improvement from time to time based on their experiences.

When a computer system is exposed to a situation repeatedly, it can show an improvement in the way it responds with time. The system is said to have learned when it shows an improvement.

The popularity of machine learning began when researchers discovered that computers can react to situations without being programmed to do so. In this book you will learn the various aspects of machine learning.

# Chapter 2

# Markov Models

A Markov model is a stochastic model used to model randomly changing systems. The assumption is that the future states are dependent on the current state, but independent of the events that happened in the past (Markov Property). Generally, this enables reasoning and computation by use of the model that would have been intractable.

Below are the four types of Markov models highly used:

1. Markov Chain - used by the autonomous systems and the ones with fully observable states.

2. Hidden Markov model - used by the autonomous systems with partially observable states.

3. Markov Decision Processes - used by the controlled systems that have fully observable state.

4. Partially observable Markov Decision - used by the controlled systems with a partially observable state.

Markov models may be expressed by use of equations or graphical models. In graphic Markov models, circles, each with states, are used. Directional arrows are used to indicate the possible transition changes between the states. The directional arrows are

normally labeled with the rate of transition.

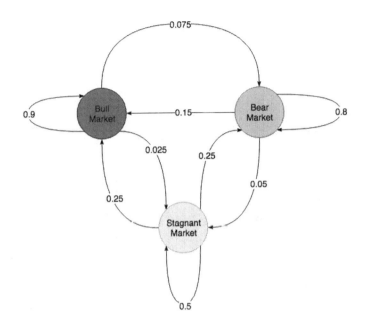

An example of Markov Chain

## The Markov Property

The Markov Property states that, "The future is

independent of the past given the present." A state

$St$ is *Markov* if and only if: $P\ [S_{t+1}\ |\ S_t] = P\ [S_{t+1}\ |\ S_1,$

..., $S_t]$ The state will capture all the relevant

information from history. After the state has been

17

known, the history can be thrown away; the state forms a sufficient statistic of the future.

## State Transition Matrix

For a Particular Markov State, $s$ and its successor state, $s'$, the state transition probability is defined as follows:

$$P_{ss'} = P\,[S_{t+1} = s' \mid S_t = s]$$

The state transition matrix P defines the transition probabilities from all the states $s$ to all the successor states $s'$...

$$\mathcal{P} \ = from \quad \begin{matrix} to \\ \begin{bmatrix} \mathcal{P}_{11} & \cdots & \mathcal{P}_{1n} \\ \vdots & & \\ \mathcal{P}_{n1} & \cdots & \mathcal{P}_{nn} \end{bmatrix} \end{matrix}$$

...in which every row of the matrix sums up to 1.

# MARKOV MODELS

## Markov Process

A Markov Process refers to a memory-less, random process, that is, sequence of random states $S_1$, $S_2$, $S_3$, … that satisfy the Markov Property.

A Markov Process/Markov Chain is a tuple *(S,P)*, where:

- *S* is a set of finite states
- *P* is a state transition probability matrix,
- $P_{ss'} = P\,[S_{t+1} = s' \mid S_t = s]$

## Markov Reward Process

A Markov Reward Process refers to a Markov Chain with values.

A *Markov Reward Process* is a tuple *(S;P;R; γ)*, where:

- *S* denotes a finite set of states
- *P* denotes a state transition probability matrix,

  $P_{ss'} = P\,[S_{t+1} = s' \mid S_t = s]$

- *R* denotes a reward function, $Rs = E[Rt+1 j St = s]$

- $\gamma$ denotes a discount factor, $\gamma \varepsilon [0, 1]$

In most cases, Markov Rewards and Decision Processes are discounted. This is due to the following reasons:

1. It is mathematically convenient to discount rewards;

2. To avoid infinite returns in cyclic Markov Processes;

3. It may be hard to fully represent uncertainty of the future;

4. For the case of financial rewards, immediate rewards may earn more interest compared to the delayed returns; and/or,

5. Human/animal behavior shows preference for an immediate reward.

# MARKOV MODELS

## Value Function

The value function, denoted as v(s) gives the long-term value of a particular state, *s*.

The state value function v(s) for a particular MRP refers to the expected return beginning from state, *s*:

$v(s) = E [Gt \mid St = s]$

## Markov Decision Process

A Markov Decision Process (MDP) refers to a Markov Reward Process with decisions. It refers to an environment in which all the states are Markov.

A Markov Decision Process is a tuple (S, A, P, R, γ):

Where:

- *S* denotes a finite set of states

- *A* denotes a finite set of actions

- *P* denotes a state transition probability matrix,

- $P^a_{ss'} = P\,[S_{t+1} = s' \mid S_t = s,\, A_t = a]$

- $R$ denotes a reward function, $R^a_s = E\,[R_{t+1} \mid S_t = s,\, A_t = a]$

- $\gamma$ is a discount factor $\gamma\,\varepsilon\,[0,\,1]$.

## Applications of Markov Models

Markov models are commonly applied in modeling of languages, image processing, natural language processing (NLP), speech recognition, bioinformatics, and in modeling of computer software and hardware systems.

# Chapter 3

# Reinforcement Learning

Reinforcement learning is a goal-oriented learning process based on interaction with the environment. It presents the best hope for true artificial intelligence. This type of machine learning is growing rapidly, leading to new algorithms that can be applied in different applications.

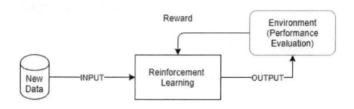

Suppose you have a pet in your home. A whistle or a clicker is a simple technique to help the pet know a treat is ready. This is "reinforcing" your pet to learn and practice some good behavior. You click the clicker then follow up with some treat.

With time, your pet will get used to the sound and will respond whenever it sounds. From this example, we can come up with the following:

1.  The pet is the artificial agent.

2.  The treat is the reward function.

3.  Good behavior is the resultant action.

# REINFORCEMENT LEARNING

This is how reinforcement learning problems work. A feedback loop is normally used to reinforce the agent. If the action is right, the agent is rewarded, and if the action is wrong, the agent is punished. Basically, the following are the components of a reinforced learning problem:

- an internal state maintained by the agent to learn about the environment;

- a reward function used to train the agent how to behave;

- an environment, which is a scenario the agent faces;

- an action performed by the agent in the environment; and/or,

- an agent that does all the deeds.

**Examples of Reinforcement Learning**

Reinforcement learning is applicable in real life problems. Generally, the start state and the end state of an agent are well known. However, there are multiple paths that lead to the end state.

This is a good scenario where reinforcement learning can be applied. Examples of applications of reinforcement learning include the driverless car, scheduling elevators, and self-navigating robot vacuum cleaners that we often see in homes.

**Reinforcement Learning Frameworks**

We need to examine an example of a reinforcement learning problem to understand how to solve reinforcement learning problems. In this case, we can use the Multi-Armed Bandit problem.

Suppose you face multiple slot machines that have random payouts. You need to get maximum bonus from your slot machines in the shortest time possible. What can you do?

Amongst the naïve approaches is to choose a single slot machine, then keep on pulling the lever all day long. The approach is tiresome, but it can give you some payouts. Yes, you may hit the jackpot, but there is a high probability you will be waiting in front of the same slot machine all the time while losing money. This can be termed a "pure exploitation" method, and not the optimal approach.

We have another approach. We can pull the lever of every slot machine hoping one of them will hit the jackpot. The approach is naïve as it can keep one pulling the levers throughout the day. The payouts from the approach will be sub-optimal. The approach is a "pure exploration approach".

The two approaches are not optimal, so we must look for a way to balance the two and get the maximum reward. This is referred to as the "exploration vs exploitation dilemma" of machine learning.

First, we should state the reinforcement learning problem framework then comes up with a list of ways to get a solution to the problem in question.

**Markov Decision Process:**

The Markov Decision Process is the mathematical framework that defines a solution in a reinforcement learning scenario. It can be stated as follows:

- Set of actions, A
- Set of states, S

- Reward function, R

- Value, V

- Policy, π

An action (A) should be taken to transition from the start state to the end state, S, and we will get a reward in return for every action taken. Note that any action taken can lead to a negative or positive reward. The "actions taken" defines the policy (π), while the rewards we earn in return define our values (V). The goal is to choose the right policy to maximize our rewards. We must maximize:

$$E(r_t \mid \pi, s_t)$$

...for values of $S$ in time, $t$.

## Traveling Salesman Problem

In the Travelling Salesman Problem, the goal is to travel from the starting point to the end point at the lowest cost possible.

Numbers are added on the edges between two points indicating the cost of traversing from one state to another. Earnings may be added in the form of negative numbers. In such a case, value is defined as the cumulative reward once a policy is done.

In the Traveling Salesman Problem:

1. The states are represented as nodes such as {A, B, C, D...}.

2. The action taken is to move from one point to another, {A->B, B->C, etc.}.

3. Reward function is the value that is represented by the edge, that is, cost.

4. The policy refers to the way the task can be accomplished, example, {A->C, C->F}.

Assuming you are at point A, the visible path will be the next destination. Only observable space is known.

# REINFORCEMENT LEARNING

You may use some greedy approach and choose the most promising possible next step.

If you are at point A, and you can move to either points B, C or D, you can choose to move to point D. Your decision should be based on the amount of reward you will get.

Now that you are at point D, your goal is to move to the next point at the lowest possible cost. This should be repeated until you reach the end state at the lowest cost possible.

At the end, you will have implemented a reinforcement learning algorithm. The algorithm is referred to as "epsilon greedy", and it is a greedy approach for solving our problem. If you need to move from the start place to the end state, you should always choose that policy.

However, you should note the policy we chose is not the optimal one. We have taken a learning approach that is based on policy, and our job is to select from the best possible policies including:

1. Policy based - in which our goal is to get the optimal policy.

2. Value based - in which the goal is to get the optimal value, that is, the cumulative reward.

3. Action based - in which the focus is to get the optimal actions at every step.

# Chapter 4

# Structured Prediction

Structured prediction is a supervised machine learning technique involving the prediction of structured objects instead of scalar, real, or discrete values.

A good example is when we need to transform a natural language into a parse tree or any other syntactic representation.

In this case, the structured output domain will be made up of all the possible parse trees.

Structured prediction problems arise in cases where we have many interrelated decisions that must be weighed against each other in a bid to arrive at a globally consistent and satisfactory solution.

In natural language processing, we are expected to construct some global, coherent analysis of a sentence, translation, or parse tree into some other language.

For the case of computational biology, we normally analyze genetic sequences to predict the 3D structure of proteins, find the global alignment of the related DNA strings, then recognize the functional portions of a genome.

34

# STRUCTURED PREDICTIONS

In computer vision, complex objects are segmented into clustered scenes, 3D shapes are reconstructed from stereo and video, and finally tracking the motion of the articulated bodies.

A structured model is defined as a scoring scheme over a set of combinatorial structures and a method that helps in finding the highest scoring structure.

The score of a model is simply the function of the weights of vertices edges or any other parts of the structure. The weights are normally represented in the form of parametric functions of a set of input features.

The following are examples of structured prediction problems:

1. Sequence labeling

Given an input sequence, generate a label sequence of equal length. Every label must be drawn from a small finite set. The problem is typified in natural language processing by a part of speech tagging.

2. Parsing

   Given an input sequence, create a tree with the yield (leaves) being the elements in the sequence; the structure should be grammatically correct. The problem is typified in natural language processing by syntactic parsing.

3. Collective classification

   Given a graph that is defined by a set of edges and vertices, produce a labeling for the vertices. The problem is normally typified by relation learning problems, like labeling web pages when given link information.

4. Bipartite matching

   Given a bipartite graph, find the best matching. In natural language processing, the problem is typified by word alignment and protein structure prediction in computational biology.

There are various other problems in natural language processing that fall under the heading of structured prediction, but they have not received much attention. Examples include automatic document summarization, entity detection and tracking, machine learning and question answering, etc.

In structured prediction, the output problems decompose into variable length vectors over a finite set.

# Chapter 5

# Naïve Bayes Classifier

Naïve Bayes is a classification that works based on the Naïve Bayes theorem, while assuming the predictors are independent.

In a Naïve Bayes classifier, it is assumed that the availability of a certain feature in a certain class is not related to the presence of any other feature. Example, an apple is fruit with a diameter of about 3cm, round, and red in color.

Although these features are dependent or rely on the presence of other features, their contributions to probability of the fruit being an apple is independent. Therefore, the classifier is called "naïve".

It's easy to build a Naïve Bayes model and use it with large datasets. This classifier is also known to be good compared to the other classification algorithms.

The Naïve Bayes classifier predicts the membership probabilities of every class like the probability of a given data point or record belonging to a certain class. The class that has the highest probability is the most likely class. This is also referred to as the Maximum A Posteriori (MAP).

# NAIVE BAYES CLASSIFIER

## How the algorithm works?

To understand how the Naïve Bayes Algorithm works, we can use an example. Suppose we have a training data set about weather and the target variable, which is "Play". Our goal is to classify/determine whether players will or won't play depending on the weather condition.

The following steps can help you perform the classification:

| Weather | Play |
|---------|------|
| Sunny | No |
| Overcast | Yes |
| Rainy | Yes |
| Sunny | Yes |
| Sunny | Yes |
| Overcast | Yes |
| Rainy | No |
| Rainy | No |

| Sunny | Yes |
|---|---|
| Rainy | Yes |
| Sunny | No |
| Overcast | Yes |
| Overcast | Yes |
| Rainy | No |

1. First, convert your dataset into frequency table. This is given below:

| Frequency Table | | |
|---|---|---|
| Weather | No | Yes |
| Overcast | | 4 |
| Rainy | 3 | 2 |
| Sunny | 2 | 3 |
| Grand Total | 5 | 9 |

2. Create a likelihood table simply by determining the probabilities, *i.e.* the Overcast probability is 0.29, playing is 0.64.

3. Use the Naïve Bayes equation to determine posterior probability for every class. A class

# NAIVE BAYES CLASSIFIER

with highest probability will be the result of the

prediction.

Suppose you have the following problem:

*The players will play on a sunny weather.*

Your task is to determine whether the statement is

correct or incorrect.

This problem can be solved using the posterior

probability method as follows:

P(Yes | Sunny) = P( Sunny | Yes) * P(Yes) / P (Sunny)

We then have the following:

P(Sunny) = 5/14 = 0.36,

 (Sunny |Yes) = 3/9 = 0.33,

P( Yes)= 9/14 = 0.64

Then,

P (Yes | Sunny) = 0.33 * 0.64 / 0.36 = 0.60

This shows it has a high probability.

In Naïve Bayes, the same approach is used for prediction of probability of a different class depending on different attributes.

## Pros of Naïve Bayes

1. It is fast, easy way to predict a class of data set for testing. It can also be applied very well in the prediction of a multi class problem.

2. When the assumption of independence is true, the Naïve Bayes classifier works very well compared to the other models. Much less training data is needed.

3. It performs better when we have categorical input variables than numerical variables. For the case of numerical variables, we need to have an assumption that there is a normal distribution.

## Cons of Naïve Bayes

1. For a categorical variable with some category that hasn't been observed in data set, the model assigns a zero-probability making it unable to generate a prediction. This is called a "Zero Frequency". The smoothing technique can be used to solve this problem. Laplace estimation can be employed to solve it.

2. Naïve Bayes is referred to as bad estimator. Sometimes the outputs it gives are not taken seriously.

3. The Naïve Bayes also assumes the predictors are independent. In a real-life situation, it's nearly impossible for us to get independent predictors.

## Applications of Naive Bayes Algorithm

The Naïve Bayes Classifier is applied in the following fields:

1. Real time Prediction

   Naïve Bayes is a faster learning classifier. This makes it applicable in making real time predictions.

2. Multi-class Prediction

   The Naïve Bayes Classifier is known to be good in multi-class prediction. We can use it for prediction of target variables of multiple classes.

3. **Text classification/Sentiment Analysis/ Spam Filtering**

   When used for text classification, Naïve Bayes Algorithm models give a high accuracy compared to the other types of models. It is also used in spam filtering to identify spam emails and in sentiment analysis, example, in social media to determine positive as well as negative customer comments.

4. Recommendation Systems

The Naïve Bayes Classifier together with Collaborative Filtering can be used to build a recommendation system that uses data mining and machine learning techniques for filtering any unseen information. It can also generate a prediction on whether a user will like or reject a resource.

# Chapter 6

## SVM

Support Vector Machine (SVM) is a very popular machine learning algorithm. The popularity of the algorithm began with its invention in 1990s and it continues to perform very well with only a little tuning.

SVM is a supervised machine learning algorithm that can be applied in both regression and classification problems. When using the algorithm, each data item is plotted in an n-dimensional space (*n* represents the number of features you have) and the value of each feature is the value of the corresponding coordinate.

Classification is then done by finding a hyper-plane that separates the two classes very well.

Support vectors are the coordinates of the individual observations. The Support Vector Machine is the frontier that best separates the two classes.

## How SVM Works

You now know how to use a hyper-plane to segregate your two classes. How can we identify the right hyper-plane?

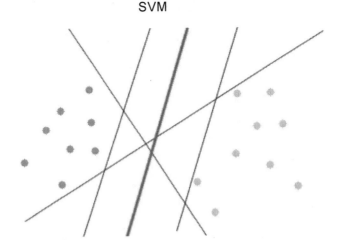

When choosing the hyper-plane, you should follow the rule of thumb, which is, "Select the hyper-plane that separates the two classes better." This makes it easy for you to choose the right hyper-plane if you more than one hyper-plane. Use your eyes and determine the one that separates them at a central point. That will be the best hyper-plane.

However, you may more than one hyper-planes, all of which separate the classes very well. In such a case, you should maximize the distance between the nearest data point in either class and the hyper-plane.

51

This distance is referred to as the "margin". Then, choose the hyper-plane with the highest margin. Another reason behind selecting a hyper-plane with a higher margin is robustness. If you choose the hyper-plane with the lowest margin, there will be a significant chance for miss-calculation.

Also, if you find that one of the hyper-planes has a classification error (it doesn't segregate the two classes well), don't use it.

You may find, however, that one data point appears in the territory of the other circle - an "outlier". SVM provides a feature for ignoring outliers and determining the hyper-plane with the maximum margin. In this case, the SVM can be said to be "robust" to outliers.

## Support Vector Machines (Kernels)

Practically, SVM is implemented using a kernel. In a linear SVM, the learning of the hyper-plane takes place by transforming the problem using linear algebra, but we will not discuss this as it is out of scope.

Linear SVM can be rephrased by use of the inner product of any two observations, instead of the observations themselves. The inner product between two vectors refers to the sum of the multiplication of every pair of input values.

Example: suppose you have the vectors [2, 3] and [5, 6], their inner product will be 2*5 + 3*6 or 28.

The equation used to make prediction for a new input by use of dot product between input (x) and every support vector (xi) can be calculated as shown below:

**f(x) = B0 + sum(ai * (x,xi))**

The equation involves calculating the inner products of a new input vector (x) with all the support vectors in the training data. The learning algorithm must estimate the coefficients, *B0* and *ai*, for every input from the training data.

## Linear Kernel SVM

The dot product is referred to as the "kernel" and can be written as follows:

**K(x, xi) = sum(x * xi)**

The kernel defines the similarity (or the distance measure) between the new data and the support vectors. A linear kernel or a linear SVM uses the dot
54

product as the similarity measure since the distance is simply a linear combination of the inputs.

There are also other kernels that can be used to transform the input space into higher dimensions like radial kernel and Polynomial kernel.

## Polynomial Kernel SVM

Instead of dot-product, we can choose to use a polynomial product. Consider the following example:

**K(x,xi) = 1 + sum(x * xi)^d**

The degree of the polynomial should be specified by hand to our learning algorithm. If the value of d=1, then it is like a linear kernel. In the polynomial kernel, curved lines are allowed in the input space.

## Radial Kernel SVM

It is possible for us to have a complex radial kernel.

Example:

**K(x,xi) = exp(-gamma * sum((x – xi^2))**

The gamma parameter should be specified to the learning algorithm. It is recommended that you use 0.1 as its value, and 0 < gamma < 1.

## Pros of SVMs

1. SVM works very well in case of smaller and cleaner datasets.

2. They provide a high degree of accuracy.

3. SVM can be more efficient since it uses a subset of training points.

## Cons of SVMs

1. It becomes less accurate when the dataset has noise and has overlapping classes.

2. It is not suitable for large datasets since the training time can be high.

## Applications of SVM

SVM can be used in text classification tasks such as detecting spam emails, category assignment, and sentiment analysis. SVM is also used in image recognition challenges, and it performs well in color-based classification and aspect-based recognition. SVM plays an important role in areas of handwritten, digit recognition like postal automation services.

# Chapter 7

# Random Forest

Random forest is a supervised machine learning algorithm. The algorithm works by creating a forest with several trees. The more trees the forest has, the more robust the forest will look. A forest with a high number of trees gives higher accuracy.

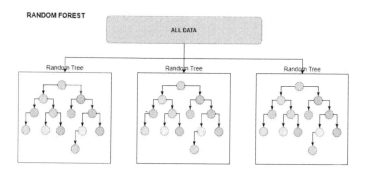

In random forest algorithm, instead of using a *gini* index or an information gain to calculate the root of a node, the process of identifying the root node and splitting the feature nodes happens automatically.

## How the Algorithm Works

The pseudo code below explains how the random forest algorithm works:

1.  Randomly choose "k" features from the total "m" features.

    Where k << m

2. From the "k" features, calculate the node "d" by use of best split point.

3. Use the best split to split the node into daughter nodes.

4. Repeat 1 to 3 steps until you reach a "l" number of nodes.

5. Build a forest by repeating steps 1 to 4 for "n" number of times to create "n" number of trees.

In the random forest algorithm, we first choose "k" features from "m" features. We then use the best split approach to find the root node of the "k" features we have selected from "m". In the next step, we use the best split approach to find the daughter nodes.

Repeat the first three steps until you get a tree with a root node and with the target as the leaf node. Finally, the steps 1 to 4 are repeated until we get "n" randomly created trees. The randomly created trees will then form our random forest.

## Application of Random Forest Algorithm

1. Banking

   In banking sector, the random forest algorithm is used to find fraudulent customers and loyal customers. The loyal customer is the one who repays loans without defaulting. This helps banks make better decisions when awarding loans.

2. Medicine

   The algorithm is used to determine the correct combination of components to validate medicine. It can also be used to identify a disease.

3. Stock Market

# RANDOM FOREST

Random forest helps to identify stock behavior and the expected loss or profit when buying a stock.

## Advantages of Random Forest Algorithm

1. It does not suffer from the overfitting problem when used to solve classification problems.
2. It can be used to solve both regression and classification problems.
3. It can be used in feature engineering in which the most important features are identified from the available features in a training set.

## Disadvantages of Random Forest Algorithm

1. Random forest models can be slow to make predictions after they have been trained.
2. More accurate ensembles normally require more trees, meaning it can be slower to use.

# Chapter 8

## Model Evaluation

It is always good to evaluate your model to determine whether it will predict the target correctly in the cases of both new and future data. The target values for your future data are unknown, hence you should use the data you have and its corresponding target values to determine the accuracy metric of your model.

The assessment should be used as a proxy for predictive accuracy on your future data.

To evaluate a model correctly, hold the data set whose target values are known. This should be obtained from the data source. It is not advisable for you to use the data that was used to train a machine learning model to test its predictive accuracy.

This will only reward models that can "remember" training data rather than drawing generalizations from it.

Once you have trained a machine learning model, the held-out observations whose target values are known should be send to the model. Then compare the results you get from the model with the target values or the known values.

If you get the difference between the two, you will be able to tell how accurate your machine learning model is. Finally, compute a summary metric telling you how true the predicted and the true values match.

## Preventing Overfitting

When you are creating and training your machine learning model, your goal should be to choose the model that makes the best predictions, which is the model displaying the best settings.

There is a danger in choosing a model's parameter settings that give the best "predictive" performance on evaluation data. You may end up "overfitting" your model.

Overfitting normally occurs when a model has memorized the patterns occurring in training and evaluation data sources, but it has failed to generalize the patterns in data. An overfitted model will perform well during evaluations, but it is unable to make accurate predictions on any unseen data.

To avoid an overfitted model, preserve some data to use in validating the performance of your machine learning model. You can choose to use 60% of your data for training, 20% of it for evaluation, and the remaining 20% for validation.

Once you have chosen the model parameters for the evaluation data, you can run a second evaluation using the validation data and see how well your machine learning model performs. If the test meets your expectations using your validation data, it is not overfitted.

# MODEL EVALUATION

If you use a third set of data for validation, you will choose the right machine learning model parameters to prevent overfitting.

However, if you keep data from training process for validation and evaluation means that you will have lesser data for training purpose.

This is a problem with using small data sets. It is always good for you to use a large data set in machine learning.

## Cross-Validation

Cross-validation refers to the process of evaluating machine learning models in which several machine learning models are trained on the subsets of the available input data, then evaluating them on complementary subset of the data. Cross-validation can be used to detect overfitting.

69

The k-fold cross validation is a nice method for cross-validation. In this method, the input data is split into $k$ subsets of data, which are also known as *folds*. A machine learning model is then trained on all except one of the data sets; that is, the training is done with $k$-1 datasets.

The evaluation of the model is then done using the subset that was not used for training. The training process is then repeated several times, using a different dataset for evaluation each time. This means the process is repeated $k$ times.

## Confidence Interval

This is a good metric for assessing the reliability of a statistical estimate. A wide confidence interval is an indication you have a poor model. If the confidence interval doesn't change after modifying the model, it means your data is very noisy.

# MODEL EVALUATION

## Confusion Matrix

This is a technique used to evaluate the prediction power of a model employing a clustering algorithm. It is an $N * N$ matrix, in which $N$ represents the cluster number.

The matrix should be designed as follows:

The element contained in cell $(i, j)$ shows the number of the observations in the data set for training that belongs to $i^{th}$ cluster and have been assigned to the cluster $j$.

After the numbers have been changed into proportions, the matrices are referred to as "contingency tables".

An observation that has been assigned incorrectly is referred to as a "false positive" or a "false negative" A higher number of observations along the diagonal of a confusion matrix indicates the model is more accurate

when making predictions.

.

# Chapter 9

# Business Applications

Machine learning is applied in businesses in various ways. Let us discuss these:

## Logistics

In logistics, all decisions are made based on forecasting. These decisions include labor staffing, inventory management, managing allocations, and container repositioning. However, the complexity of this industry is increasing, making forecasting inadequate.

Bad forecasts lead to poor planning and inefficiencies, which in turn leads to under-utilized or misallocate resources and poor customer service provision and trade management. The traditional methods employed by industry to bring efficiencies have not yielded good returns.

For air shipping and courier companies to earn profits, they must be smarter. The use of predictive logistics technology is influenced by proprietary machine learning and customized for container freight. Proper information facilitates in driving true intelligence and helps to solve operational and commercial challenges for carriers and non-vessel operating carriers, third-party logistics providers, freight forwarders, shippers, marine terminal operators, fourth party logistics providers, and others.

There is a growth of interest in machine learning, and it is now used to gather and analyze logistics data to provide ways for the container shipping industry to create accurate plans.

Shippers, carriers, and freight forwarders are now able to make more informed decisions by use of machine learning techniques. These decisions help to optimize the travel time, costs, and resources required to move the cargo.

## Transportation

Machine learning is very applicable in the transport sector. A good example is Uber, which offers taxi services in most countries in the world.

Uber has extensively applied machine learning techniques and the application of analytics tools for big data. This has played a great role in the success of the company.

When Uber was moving its customers from one point to another point, it was collecting information at the same time regarding customers' choices and behaviors.

This has helped the company to identify its customers at an individual level. Knowing places customers like to go as well as the joints they like visit, Uber was able to elevate its services to a level much higher than other companies.

Uber has even partnered with hotels and provides discounts when offering their services. Many industries including restaurants, airports, tourist destinations, and others now promote Uber. That is what machine learning can do to a business.

Machine learning and big data are expected to bring many changes to the transport sector. Consider the case of a driverless car. Other ideas and concepts that are now on the drawing board are expected to be implemented and they will impact the transport sector.

In Singapore, a machine learning program is used to predict the use of public transportation. The program is based on the distribution of amenities and land use in Singapore.

Video surveillance, which is part of the transport sector has greatly benefitted from machine learning. Machine learning has been used to implement systems able to detect any anomalies in the flow of traffic. By use of machine learning algorithms, the systems can observe the movements of cars and spotting any anomalies such as accidents, congestion, or pedestrians crossing the road incorrectly.

## Financial

Machine learning has really impacted the financial sector. By use of automated trading, which is also known as algorithmic trading, human bias that can lead to losses, is eliminated.

Fear and greed can accentuate the likelihood of loss. When machine learning is implemented in the stock market, we can be certain we will end up winning the game.

The most prominent hedge funds in the world use machine learning for algorithmic trading. These have

78

been using this technology for a long period of time. A good example of this is Medallion Fund at Renaissance.

High frequency trading involves the use of technology to disrupt antiquated business lines that drag the investor's earnings. From this, we can learn how machine learning and artificial intelligence can be used to reduce the friction involved in the trading process. Machine learning can lead to ease in finding customers.

## Banking

Machine learning is widely applied in the banking sector. Consider data security, which is an issue of concern in the banking industry.

Cyber security experts have stated that new malware is made of code closely related to the previous versions. With this knowledge, machine learning can be used to identify any anomalies in user behavior and network traffic making it easier for banks to analyze and detect any legitimate attacks on their resources.

Even in areas like compliance, machine learning can be used for infusion of automation and run tasks that adhere to changing regulatory protocols with ease.

Banking chatbots rely on machine learning to study and understand customer behavior and to track their spending habits. The banks also rely on machine learning to recommend how customers can manage their finances.

Erica, which is a chatbot for Bank of America, helps customers perform their banking transactions while giving insights on how to manage their finances.

## BUSINESS APPLICATIONS

Machine learning is also used to promote products and services and to provide targeted offers to the customers, which leads to increased customer satisfaction.

Machine learning helps banks in near real-time fraud detection. This becomes very important to banks considering the amount of money banks are losing to bank fraud. Machine learning can be used in banks to detect patterns from the historical behavior of account owners.

Whenever an uncharacteristic transaction occurs, a notification can be generated to alert the bank and the account owner of the possibility of fraud. This can also be used as an anti-money laundering tool to trace the source of money and to prevent the flow of illegal cash.

Banks are also looking for ways to come up with improved loan approval processes. Machine learning can be used in this area. Knowledge can be gathered from spending habits, credit scores, financial data, etc.

Machine learning algorithms can rely on this data to generate risk scores and to predict the possibility of a user defaulting on a loan. When banks are equipped with such information, it becomes easy for them to come up with terms and conditions for different customers with different profiles.

Machine learning algorithms are capable of processing large amounts of datasets. Subsequently, they can predict stock market trading based on volatility patterns, latest news, risks, etc. Investment banks have leveraged machine learning algorithms to help track trading volatility, to support equity trade, and to support wealth and asset management. They also rely on machine learning algorithms to decide how to allocate funds to customers in different trading blocks, then process and execute them. This can reduce the amount of time it takes to execute custom trades.

## Currencies

Machine learning algorithms can be used to predict the flow of currency between various markets. A good example is currency-prediction.com that predicts the flow of money and separates the predictable part of the assets from stochastic noise.

A model is then created that can project the future trajectory of a market on the multidimensional space of the other markets. The system will give the predicted trend in the form of a number, either positive or negative, together with a wave chart predicting how the waves will overlap the trend. This can help the trader to know the time to enter the market, the time to exit the market, and the direction to trade.

One of the good features of any trading system is the ability to predict where the price will fall. Machine learning algorithms can help to create systems with this capability. Based on the historical data, a system can be implemented that will predict where the price will fall after a period.

This will help a trader make wise decisions when trading. Note that for this to be achieved, some indicators should be used. The indicators should have the capability of predicting some short-term price movements.

Each indicator used should can show whether the market is going up or down making it easier to predict the price in the future.

## Gaming

Computers have shown the ability to learn how to play games well. This can easily be implemented by use of reinforced learning algorithms that normally learn by playing a game.

An example is a bot that presses buttons randomly while targeting to hit a ball. This bot should be trained to observe its actions and the rewards it gets.

In programming, the algorithm is informed of what is expected, like completing the game with a score of at least 100. The algorithm will then try different combinations randomly, learning with time until the desired goal is reached.

Games based on machine learning should have a performance analyzer. This should be responsible for judging the performance of the agent against a suitable performance measure, and it should not confine itself to the behavior that was observed recently.

The learning agent involved in the game should not be left to work or determine how to play on its own. It should be provided with an amount of prior knowledge about the way it should behave.

Most game developers have been using machine learning algorithms to create a better computer player artificial agent. Once the agent has won a game, it should not continue to follow the way or method that led it to win the game. It should be able to explore new ways of winning games.

With reinforcement learning, it is easy to implement games utilizing the concept of machine learning. Although currently not many games have been developed, reinforcement learning is a very promising field for game development.

## Human Resources

Machine learning is transforming human lives both at home and at work. Maybe you use the Alexa to control lighting, open and close doors, unlock your car, etc.

Machine learning is assisting people at their work places and helping them work smarter. CEO's and managers need to know what is really happening in their companies, especially on the part of their employees.

Leaders and executives need information that will help them point people in the right directions. With machine learning, companies can extract trends and patterns from data in the shortest time possible, an activity that can take days when attempted by human beings. Some of these patterns may end up not uncovered at all.

Machine learning can be applied in the hiring process of any organization. Suppose we have a company that receives tens of thousands of resumes every year. The company also makes thousands of hires every year. Half work – the others fail.

The company keeps track of who sees their job ads and how the ads are viewed. Consequently, the company can analyze and categorize the data contained in the resumes. It can also obtain and keep data about the social media activity of the applicants.

In short, every piece of data regarding the applicant is kept well.

The data is then fed into a machine learning software on a continual basis. Patterns will emerge.

The software finds that a job advert and website yield more successful hires. One interviewer is better in identifying talent than others. Individuals using a specific social media platform make better employees. Such information proves very beneficial and reveals individual patterns and other pertinent factors.

Only a software that uses the concept of machine learning can extract such information from data. An HR professional is unable to do everything. A traditionally coded software is also unable to do this. When a machine learning software is utilized properly, an organization make the best hiring decisions in terms of quality and suitability.

Employee attrition and subsequent employee turnover are also areas of concern. The true costs of high turnover have become widely known and companies are doing as much as they can to stop the bleeding of talent.

Even after appropriate internal communication, it becomes hard to perform a comprehensive analysis of people's statements, intentions, questions, and decisions, all of which can lead to employee attrition. A human HR professional cannot do everything.

However, when using a machine learning software, some of the patterns become identifiable. Responses on employee satisfaction surveys for example and drops in efficiency be precursors to employee attrition. There are numerous signals that only become important in certain combinations, patterns that are difficult for a human being to spot.

Machine learning has also shown its potential in boosting individual skill management and development. This field is still developing; platforms capable of giving calibrated guidance with no human coaches provide an opportunity for saving time and enabling more people can grow their careers and to stay engaged.

A good example is Workday, which builds personalized training recommendations for the employees based on the market trends, needs, and specifications of the employees in the company.

# Chapter 10

## Recommender Systems

Recommendation engines are a form of an automated "shop counter guy". You can ask him for a product. He shows you the item as well as the related ones you can buy. Recommendation engines are trained very well in cross selling and up selling. This is how recommender systems work.

The systems analyze your past behavior then create a recommendation. They bring customers delight and gives them a good reason to return to the website.

## Types of Recommendation Engines

Before discussing the various types of recommendation engines, let us explore some of the intuitive recommendations we can make.

Consider the scenarios given below:

1. Recommending the most popular items

   A basic approach is to recommend the items a lot of users like. However, there is a major drawback with this approach – no personalization.

   The popularity of an item will be defined based on the entire pool, meaning that the most popular items will be the same for every user.

# RECOMMENDER SYSTEMS

A website recommends you buy a refrigerator because other users have liked it, but it doesn't care whether you are interested in buying the appliance or not.

This approach works very well in news portals. After logging into a news portal such as bbcnews, you will see a section for *Popular News*. It is subdivided into subsections and displays the most popular articles most prominently.  The approach works very well.

2.  Using a Classifier for Recommendation

There are various classification algorithms. These can be used for recommendation purposes.

Classifiers are normally based on parameters, so we must define the parameters (features) of both the item and the user. The outcome will be 1 if the user likes it and 0 in case the user doesn't.

This approach incorporates personalization and it can be applied even in circumstances where the history of the user is very short. However, the approach also has some drawbacks that limit its usefulness.

We might not have the features, or we might not have a sufficient amount to construct the classifier. As the number of items and users increase, it will become exponentially difficult to make a good classifier.

## Recommendation Algorithms

There is a special class of algorithms made specifically for solving recommendation problems.

Let us discuss these:

1. **Context Based Algorithms**

   These algorithms are based on driving the context of an item. After gathering the context level information about the item, you search for the look-alike items and recommend them.

   A good example is on YouTube: you can find the language, genre, and starring of a video. Based on this information, we can find the look-alike of this video or the ones that are related.

   After getting the look-alike, we can recommend

them to a customer who had originally seen only the first video. Such algorithms are very popular in online music stores, video online channels, etc. Such context level information is easy to get when the item/product can be explained using only few dimensions.

## 2. Collaborative Filtering Algorithms

This is a very popular algorithm due to the fact it does not depend on any additional information.

You are only required to have the transaction level information of the industry. Corporations such as American Express and e-commerce players such as Amazon use these algorithms to make recommendations of their products.

# RECOMMENDER SYSTEMS

Collaborative filtering algorithms can be classified into three categories as follows:

- *User-User Collaborative Filtering* - in this case, we find a look-alike customer, then offer the products the original customer selected.

  The algorithm is very effective, but it consumes a lot of resources and takes a long time to determine each customer pair information.

  Therefore, for the case of big base platforms, it is hard to implement an algorithm without a strong parallelizable system.

- *Item-Item collaborative filtering* - this is closely related to the previous algorithm, but instead of looking for the customer look-alikes, we look for the item look-alikes.

After getting the item look-alike matrix, it becomes easy to recommend similar items to a customer who has purchased something.

When compared to the previous algorithm, the item-item collaborative filtering consumes fewer resources and less time since all the similarity scores between the customers are not needed. With a fixed number of items, the product-product look alike matrix will remain fixed over some time.

- *Other simpler Algorithms*

   Market basket analysis is one of them, but its predictive power is not strong compared to the previous two.

# Chapter 11

# Datasets

Before beginning a machine learning project, most people experience the problem of getting some good datasets. Finding a good machine learning dataset is essential to getting actionable insights.

Some companies believe they must collect their own data to be able to benefit from big data. This is not true. Currently, there are several datasets available, and these can be used and analyzed by anyone who is willing to look at them. Let us discuss some of the datasets that are available to the public:

1.  **/r/datasets**

    The /r/datasets provided by Reddit provide machine learning experts with a social way by which they can share and request datasets. Here, you can find many datasets, with links to datasets for deep learning. They have unorganized and random collection of datasets, and yield very serendipitous finds.

2.  ***Natural Earth Data***

    This has a geospatial dataset that has been optimized to be used in applications for web mapping. The datasets have map data in vector layers and raster data layers. They are countries, cultural data, boundary lines, water boundaries, population attribution, and more. Vector data exists as ESRI shape files and raster data exists in the TIFF format. It makes it possible to integrate the mapping utilities to web or native applications.

### 3. UC Irvine

The UCI Repository is well-known and highly used. It has various datasets that can be used in AI applications. In this repository, the datasets are grouped by task (such as classification, regression, etc.), data type (such as time-series, multivariate, etc.), and more.

Some of the most common datasets include the GPS trajectories, air quality in Italy, and student alcohol consumption. Other interesting datasets in this repository are the Abalone physical characteristics, chemical composition from Italy-grown wine, and heart disease data. Each data set provided in the repository comes with very useful metadata, such as information regarding data sources, data types, relevant papers, etc. The data sets are provided in various formats including .ZIP and .CSV.

### 4. *Google Trends Datastore*

The data source is very good for exploratory exercises by use of search queries with time. Google Trends gives the trending queries via interest with time, regional maps, visualizations, and history of queries.

You can refine your searches based on categories, regions, like businesses, sports, entertainment, and others. It is interesting to see how the varying trends relate to each other with time, like determining how the climate change, recession, global warming, and economy queries compare with each other for the past five years.

You can look at the trending data on the home page in real-time. All the data is provided in the form of a CSV value.

5. *Machine Learning Data Set Repository*

This has data sets ranging from network analytics data to labor strike data. They also include the like licensing, metadata, attribute types, and dependencies.

The data is also provided in various formats including .ZIP, .CSV, .TAR and .XML. The datasets are categorized, searchable, and labeled with download counts, star ratings, and comments, making it easy for you to find the dataset you need.

## 6. *USGS.gov*

The U.S Geological Survey is a good source of geological data and natural resources. It explores topics including biology, climate change, and mineral data.

The site provides its users with access to scientific research data, real-time data, and GIS datasets. The website also provides its users with access to numerous endpoints including Waterservices API, which provides catalog tool for data that can be used for browsing through the geological and natural resources data.

The datasets from data catalogs includes groundwater depletion, biodiversity counts, geothermal data, etc.

Every data portal has rich metadata and it is provided in shape files in .ZIP format or raster dataset in .GXF format. The non-GIS data is normally provided in the XML, CSV, JSON formats, and others.

## 7. *Deep Learning Datasets*

It is a very effective source of data for machine learning problems related to deep learning. The datasets include numerous things including symbolic music, text, faces, and speech.

Most of them are well-known, including the MNIST and Penn Treebank. It is always good to keep these datasets for deep learning in one place.

## 4. *Pew Research Center Datasets*

The Pew Research Center has demographics and social trends with datasets on science, tech, religion, politics, and media fields. These datasets for machine learning are dependent on surveys, citizen polls, and questionnaires.

For you to be allowed to download these datasets, you must fill out an application form and agree to their terms and conditions. The datasets are obtained from polls; hence, they are made up of unstructured and Boolean text data.

## 5. *Open Data Network (Socrata)*

The Socrata Open Data Network is a good platform where one can get data from the government. As usual, government websites are hard to navigate, and the Socrata API provides users with an easy way to navigate through various government datasets. Not all datasets, regions, and agencies are available.

The Socrata API is also good when you need to query specific questions like, "What is the population in New York?" This will give you the population data accompanied by a map. The API will also allow you to compare the dataset with similar towns in the country, and it provides the users with questions about the location in the query.

## 6. *Open Data Stack Exchange*

The Stack Exchange has a section known as "Open Data". In this section, you can post your question and ask where you can get a r dataset. An answer will be provided.

You will find an aggregate of questions that have been posted providing methods of getting new datasets. The queries regarding where to get various datasets include data sources for disease counts, physical data for soccer players, and others. However, note that not all the posted questions are answered.

## 7. *Data is Plural*

This is a datasheet with links that lead to interesting data sources and data sets. The sheet is updated on a regular basis and those interested can access it regularly by subscribing to the newsletter. The links to the data sources include Flint water samples and each place name in US.

These are just some of the sources of datasets for machine learning. You can visit the websites and search for the dataset you desire.

# Chapter 12

## Degree Programs

You may need to engage in the study of machine learning or data science. Perhaps you are seeking a career in machine learning or data science. There are many options for you in terms of training and academic material. There are numerous options – you might want to "test drive" a few before you make a final decision.

You may be aware of the specific subject areas in which you need to major. There are various institutions offering programs in machine learning, including degree, Master's and Ph.D. programs.

Let us discuss these institutions:

1. **Georgia Tech**

   The Center for Machine Learning at the Georgia Tech is an Interdisciplinary Research Center. It is both a home for thought leaders and a training ground for the next generation of pioneers.

   The machine learning field crosses a wide variety of disciplines that use data to find patterns in the way living systems like human beings and artificial systems like robots are constructed.

The machine learning system may be designed and developed to analyze medical data or to model a financial market, but in all cases, machine learning learns from both theory and algorithm to understand the world that is surrounding us and to create the tools that we need.

At Georgia Tech, you can study a Master's degree program in machine learning. In is the 9th best institute in offering artificial intelligence programs according to *US News*.

## 2. Columbia University

It has been ranked the 15th best institution in offering artificial intelligence programs by *US News*. They offer a Master's degree program in machine learning.

The machine learning program is for students who want knowledge in machine learning techniques and applications. Machine learning is a rapidly growing field with diverse applications in bioinformatics, intelligent systems, perception, fraud detection, information retrieval, finance, and other areas.

**3. University of North Carolina - Chapel Hill**

Here, you will study various problems that combine differing types of measurements with equally prior complex knowledge, which normally pose unique challenges in machine learning.

You will learn modeling paradigms like Bayesian nonparametric methods and inference methodologies like variation methods, MCMC, and convex optimization.

*US News* has ranked UNC-CH as 25th in terms

of offering quality artificial intelligence courses.


## 4. Carnegie Mellon University

This institution has received recognition for

having the first machine learning department in

the world. At the Carnegie Mellon University

School of Computer Science (SCS), you will

work with Computer Science faculty and

alumni like William "Red" Whittaker who led

Tartan Racing team to victory in the DARPA

Grand Challenge of 2007 and is currently

leading a graduate team is competing for

Google Lunar X Prize.


These are just some of the advantages of

studying at this institution. SCS has Master's

and Ph.D. degree programs that have been ranked high in specialty and interdisciplinary areas like machine learning, systems, artificial intelligence, and theory.

## 5. South Methodist University

SMU offers DataScience@SMU, which is a Master's of Science in Data Science program and it is designed to suit working professionals.

The program has an interdisciplinary and project-based curriculum capable of helping students to build analytical, in-demand, and communication skills necessary for management of large data sets.

Students can attend in-person immersion and take part in weekly, live online classes to understand strategic behavior, statistics as well as data visualization. GRE waivers are also available for experienced applicants.

6. **University of California - Berkeley**

The University offers a Master's of Information and Data Science program that fits individuals who needs to understand problem solving in field of data science. Students learn the lifecycle of data by use of the latest methods and tools available. All the coursework is offered online, but the students should go for a 4-5-day session for immersion at UC Berkeley campus. The program takes about 12 to 20 months.

## 7. Illinois Institute of Technology

Illinois has a Master's degree program in Data Science teaching students learn how to develop machine learning models that learn from historical data. IIT has both an online and part-time option, and the program takes 12 to 16 months.

The program prepares the students for careers in data science through a thorough training covering both theory and practice. In addition to the technical material, the course includes other subjects that are important in life. These include project management, communications, and ethics. It also includes a practicum project in which the students work with various companies in a wide variety of fields.

The fact that the institution provides both online and part-time options makes it a good fit for the students who need to study while continuing with their jobs.

## 8. Indiana University, Bloomington

Indiana University offers a Data Science program with full-time, part-time, and online options. The program is unique in that it provides its students with both a technical path and a decision-maker path.

The technical course covers areas such as cloud computing, analysis of algorithms, and security of networked systems. The decision-maker field covers areas such as project management and driving changes in an organization by use of data. The various modes of study for the program makes it a bit flexible. For a blended option, one must complete 12 credits online and 18 credits on campus.

Bloomington has a good reputation in computer science and quantitative analysis, and it provides students with a good opportunity and areas in which they can do a research. The School of Informatics and Computing has 15 research centers, including the ones dealing with cybersecurity, bioinformatics, social informatics, and many other topics.

9. **New York University**

This Institution offers a Master's Degree in Data Science on a full-time basis only. It works with many colleges and schools across NYU's organization to help the University in its data science efforts. The University works closely with two centers: The Center for the Promotion of Research Involving Innovative Statistical Methodology and the Center for Urban Science and Progress.

The MS in Data Science has a capstone project that helps the students to apply the knowledge they have learned in classroom to a real-life problem.

## 10. Northwestern University

The Institution offers a Master's in Analytics (MSiA) program on a full-time basis, taking 15 months. The program was first offered in 2012, and it combines mathematics, statics, and advanced IT with data analysis. In addition to the courses, students are expected to go for an eight-month industry practicum.

In this case, a team of students must analyze the data supplied by a client, then deliver a report with recommendations in spring quarter.

The students must also go for a summer internship, which takes three months, during which they spend time in a professional setting, either single or grouped into a team of students.

A capstone design project is also involved. In this project, students work as a team during their final quarter to provide a solution to a problem provided by a company.

## 11. Rutgers University

The University offers a Master's of Business and Science program that concentrates in Analytics, Discovery Informatics, and Data Sciences. The program is offered in both full-time and part-time basis.

The program combines the fields of machine learning, computation, data management, and statistics. The program prepares students for careers as data mining engineers, predictive modelers, and data analysts for a wide variety of industries.

The curriculum has eight analytics courses (four required and four elective), and six business courses.

The required topics normally cover database systems, statistics, programming, analytic, and data mining.

The science electives cover courses in artificial intelligence, information science, computational science, or distributed computing. Most of the courses are offered at the New Brunswick campus, but some are also offered at Newark and Camden.

## 12. Stanford University

The University offers a Master's of Science in Statistics: Data Science. The program has resulted from a collaboration between Institute for Computational and Mathematical Engineering and Department of Statistics.

The core course is made up of mathematics and computer programming, but there are plenty of electives.

The electives tackle a lot of interdisciplinary subjects including human neuroimaging methods, geostatistics, computer graphics, etc. Some students normally proceed from this program to a Ph.D.

The location of Stanford in the Silicon Valley has many benefits associated with it. Students can use the Amazon EC2 platform to perform large-scale computing. The Institution has a good reputation. It frequently appears in the *U.S. News & World Report* rankings as number 1 in its Computer Science and Statistics programs. Stanford really impresses employers.

## 13. Texas A&M University

Texas A&M offers a Master's of Analytics program through its Department of Statistics. The *US News & World Report* has ranked the university at number 12. The department has been ranked as the 3<sup>rd</sup> largest in the country.

The students are also granted access to the courses at Mays Business School.

The students are trained through a predictive analysis and intensive statistical modelling course with the aim of producing the next generation of statistical innovators in the field of data science. The program is offered on a part-time basis for five semesters, and the courses are held in the evenings in City Centre Educational Facility in Houston, TX.

## 14. University of California - San Diego

The University offers a Master's of Advanced Study in Data Science and Engineering. The program is designed to suit individuals who work with large amounts of datasets.

It is a good program for individuals who are working in a technical position or those who need to change their careers to data science.

The program is offered on a part-time basis for two years, during which a total of 38 units must be covered. The courses are taught on alternating weekends, on a Friday/Saturday schedule, and the instructional materials are provided online. Most of the students who take this course are engineers with an experience of not less than two years.

The program is career focused, with the curriculum being built on the fundamentals of data science such as analysis, programming, systems, and machine learning. In the second year of study, the students are expected to come up with a project about data science and machine learning.

The findings of the project must be explained in an oral presentation. A demo of a working prototype may also be needed.

## 15. University of Minnesota -Twin Cities

The University has a Master's of Data Science program that takes a period of two years, during which 31 credits must be taken. The program is offered on a full-time basis only.

The curriculum has three required tracks, that is, algorithms, stats and infrastructure, and large-scale computing and many electives must be explored.

A capstone project covering both years is required. Research opportunities are available in various areas and industries, including big data processing in mobile cloud platforms to comparison of climate simulation model performances.

The degree program involves an interdisciplinary approach, meaning the students have access to various activities within the campus, especially in the public health. Example, the University's Institute of Health Informatics has teams of researchers who work on natural language processing.

## 16. University of Virginia

UVA has a Master's of Science program in Data Science offered on a full-time basis only. It takes 11 months to complete.

The curriculum for the program emphasizes an integrated and team-based approach. The first semesters of the course emphasize computation, languages and linear modeling.

Once the students are done with this, they go for practice and the capstone project. Graduate students have opportunities to work on the interdisciplinary data science projects. They can also enjoy training programs and the high computation resources.

The students can participate in research that is related to data integration, ethics, systems biology, law, and other subjects. Each year, the University hosts the Datapalooza, which is a University-wide showcase for research.

## 17. University of Washington - Seattle Campus

The University of Washington offers a Master's of Data Science program in its Seattle campus. The students can choose either one or two courses in data science for every quarter, and they must attend classes for one or two evenings every week.

Students work on engineering and data analysis practicum projects in groups. They must also go through all the required data science courses. At the end of the course, a capstone project must be completed.

The University has been ranked in the Top 10 Universities for Statistics and Computer Science by *U.S. News & World Report.* There is a great focus on using advanced computing tools and methods to solve real-world problems.

## 18. University of Wisconsin

The University offers a Master's of Science in Statistics: Data Science program on a full-time basis only for a period of 12 months, during which 30 credits must be completed.

The program suits working professionals who need to climb to leadership positions. The curriculum for the course covers statistics, models, complex data analysis, communication skills, and data visualizations.

By the end of the course, the students have learned a great deal in a short time.

# Chapter 13

## Online Learning

There are various institutions offering online courses in machine learning. You can register and study online with such institutions and you will earn your degree in machine learning.

Before registering for such a program, it will be good for you to know the amount of time it will take you to complete the course.

Different institutions use different methods to facilitate online learning. Before committing, ensure you will be studying at a reputable institution.

It will also be good for you to search and see how the university has been ranked in computer science, quantitative analysis, and statistics as well as the awards the institution has earned about online offerings.

Let us discuss such institutions:

1.  **Northwestern University**

    Northwestern University offers a Master's of Science in Predictive Analytics (MSPA) program.

    The program was launched in 2011 and it covers areas such as predictive modeling, data mining, and advanced statistics, but it also helps students learn business skills such as communication skills and project management with the goal of helping the students to come up with business projects related to data science.

Students should complete an overall of 11 courses, 7 required courses and 2 elective courses. The 2 electives include a leadership course and a capstone or thesis project.

2. **University of Illinois at Urbana-Champaign**

   UI offers a Professional Master's of Computer Science in Data Science. The program is offered online, and the students obtain lessons via the MOOC platform of Coursera.

However, projects, exams, and assignments must be run through the University's departments and schools. Every credit-bearing course has two Coursera MOOC classes (each taking 4-6 weeks) and an extra "high-engagement" component.

The students must learn the fundamentals such as information systems, artificial intelligence, systems networking, and data visualizations before they can be permitted to take advanced electives.Also, the curriculum has a cloud computing or data mining project.

The UI at Urbana-Champaign has been ranked at position 5 in Computer Science by *U.S. News & World Reports.*

## 3. University of Wisconsin

The University of Wisconsin offers an online Master's of Science in Data Science program. The tuition fee remains flat, regardless of whether you live in Wisconsin or out-of-state, and there are no set meeting times for the courses.

The course targets all the hot points of data science including prescriptive analytics, data mining, statistical analysis, etc. They have a virtual lab through which students can access software tools and programming languages like Python, R, Tableau, and SQL Server for free. The course has a total of 36 units.

4. **Nottingham Trent University**

Nottingham Trent University has an online program in MBA with Analytics. The program provides a flexible and convenient mode of study for the busy adults.

By the end of the course, a student acquires both business and technical skills in data science and machine learning.

# Chapter 14

# Career Opportunities

**What are the prospects of machine learning?**

Machine learning is a good tool we can apply to solve classification problems. A skill is required in the ability to come up with fundamental innovations in machine learning then apply them to solve practical problems.

There are several machine learning skills currently in high demand in the global marketplace. The most required skill is to come up with machine learning innovations then use them to solve real life problems.

For an AI career about research, a Ph.D. in machine learning is required. You also need to prove your competence in research by showing the papers you have published, peer acceptance, and implemented solutions. For those good in research, the sky is the limit, and you can earn a seven-figure salary (USD).

People capable of implementing practical solutions (especially in collaboration with cutting edge research teams) also have a bright future in machine learning.

For you to secure a job in machine learning, you should have extensive job experience and string skills in software development. You should be able to build quality systems that can be used in a production environment for industrial big data and have deep

knowledge of Python or R programming language (not

just the basics that help you put a model on some toy

data set). However, today, there is a lot of effort to

train "machine learning engineers" with this superficial

level of expertise.

Machine learning has progressed over the past few

decades, from laboratory curiosity to a technology that

can be used practically in the commercial sector. Of all

the fields of artificial intelligence, machine learning is

widely used for development of practical software

applications for computer vision, natural language

processing, speech recognition, robot control as well

as in other applications.

Most AI systems developers believe, in many

applications, it is easy to train a system by giving it

examples of the desired input-output behavior instead of programming it manually by anticipating the desired response for all the possible inputs.

The effect of machine learning has also been felt in computer science as well as across other industries that are concerned with data-intensive issues like consumer services, control of logistics chains, and the diagnosis of faults in complex systems.

Cosmology, biology, and the social sciences use machine learning extensively. Machine learning methods have been developed to analyze the high-throughput experimental data in many ways.

As the popularity of machine learning and big data has increased, many people have tried to venture into the machine learning field by taking short training courses, coding boot camps, and MOOCs. If you need to secure a career in machine learning, you must be well-skilled in computer programming and data analysis and statistics to succeed.

There is also a high demand for individuals who possess production level software development skills, but they have enough knowledge about machine learning to manipulate and draw patterns and trends from large data sets.

You may begin with skills in data analysis and statistics, then learn Python or R tools that are used for the analysis of large data sets. This way, you can address questions based on data and construct data-driven solutions to complex arguments. These skills are highly required in MBA instead of MS programs, and they are in high demand.

What does the future holds?

Machine learning has a very bright, long-term future. The world is being reshaped by machine learning. We do not need to train computers on how to do complex tasks such as text translation or image recognition; we can create systems that can learn how to it by themselves.

Deep learning, which is one of the most popular machine learning techniques in use today, helps us to build a very complex mathematical structure known as a neural network based on large quantities of data. The neural networks have been designed to work in the same way that a human brain works, and they were invented in 1930s.

However, these have become useful after the increase in the popularity of computers.

# CAREER OPPORTUNITIES

Google has employed machine learning to implement Tensorflow, a software application used by researchers at the company who need to know the powerful models that they create.

Machine learning is still a complex field. Currently, there is nothing much you can do with neural networks unless you have strong skills in coding. Machine learning enables idea sharing in a big way.

Every major implementation in machine learning is made available for free use and modification, making it possible for one to set up a simple machine learning intelligence with only a laptop and a web connection.

For machine learning to succeed, there must be data availability. Cloud storage and the digital data follow Moore's Law. The data available in the world doubles every two years, and the cost of storing the data reduces by the same rate. With such a high volume of data, more features are made available, and it is possible for more machine learning models.

This trend of increase in volumes and reduction in the storage cost is expected to continue, meaning that machine learning is a very promising field.

However, even when we have data, it is worthless unless we can leverage it. With algorithms, we can scale the manual process of managing business processes effectively.

It is predicted that we will have an algorithm economy in the future, where everything will be managed by data and algorithms. The algorithm marketplaces will function as the global meeting place for researchers, organizations, and engineers to create, remix and share the algorithmic intelligence at scale. Algorithms can be combined for manipulation of data and extraction of useful insights.

With more data becoming available, and the cost of storage going down, machine learning is beginning to move to the cloud, in which a scalable web service is simply a call to an API. Data scientists will no longer be required to implement custom code or to manage infrastructure.

The systems will then scale for them, while generating new models and delivering faster and more accurate results. It is also becoming easy to implement machine learning models.

Many machine learning platforms that host machine learning models are emerging, making it easier for companies to get started with machine learning and allowing them to move applications from a prototype to production.

## Which Industries have High Demand for Machine Learning Qualifications?

Machine learning jobs pay well. It has been predicted that by 2020, the annual demand for data developers, data scientists, and data engineers will reach 700,000.

Machine learning, data science, and big data skills are very difficult for a company to recruit, a situation with a high potential of creating a disruption in the market regarding ongoing product development and go-to-market strategies.

## CAREER OPPORTUNITIES

Organizations encounter high costs when hiring machine learning professionals. There is also a strong need for new training programs.

Machine learning, data science, and big data are the new growth areas of advance technology with shortage of trained talents. Thus, employers face the challenges of improving productivity and hiring the right talents for the company.

It is hard to find the best candidate for a data science job – it takes five more days compared to finding the best candidates for jobs in other fields. Although it is hard to find an individual qualified for such jobs, companies are ready and willing to pay premium salaries to the individuals with expertise. The pay is even higher compared to individuals experienced in Data Science.

Most jobs in data science and analytics require individuals who have gone through advanced education. So, professionals in this field ask for higher pay. Advanced analyst positions require an individual with a Ph.D. or Master's degree. A significant reward awaits if you continue learning and acquiring new skills in machine learning and data science.

Research has also shown it is hard to hire an individual for an Analytics Manager position as it takes 53 more days compared to hiring for other positions in a company. However, it is easy to recruit a Data Analyst and Science professional in the finance industry. This is also the case with the manufacturing industry.

There is a high demand for Data Science and Analytics professionals in Finance, Insurance, and IT companies. In the case of Finance and Insurance companies, Machine Learning and Data Science careers account for 19% of all the openings.

Professional service industries represent 18% of the job openings in data science. IT companies have a 17% demand for machine learning jobs. Google, Apple, and IBM are the leading companies in hiring machine learning experts. Machine learning is used in fields such as advertising, health care, agriculture, and transportation.

Even though they often lack adequate knowledge of what they need, financial institutions have the required cash to hire data science professionals.

### The Job Roles and likely Progression

Organizations across the world are generating a lot of data every day, but they are struggling to find ways of benefiting from the data. The data science teams in a company are presented with a lot of problems.

They may be required to analyze the tweets sent to a company (whether they are positive or negative), or to determine the source of sales.

Different organizations will have different data problems, and the complexity varies from one problem to another. This requires data science teams to have adequate skills.

Data science teams must come together to solve organization problems. Everyone plays a role by providing the skills to address the problem.

Let us discuss the various roles individuals play when solving a machine learning problem:

## 1. Data Scientists

Some data scientists are responsible for fine tuning the mathematical and statistical models that are applied to data.

When one is applying theoretical knowledge of algorithms and statistics to help in solving a machine learning problem, he/she is playing the role of a data scientist.

Suppose you create a machine learning model that will predict the number of default credit cards in the next month, you are serving as a data scientist.

A data scientist can take a business problem and transforming it into a data question, then creating a model that answers the question and tells a story about the findings. Data scientists act as the bridge between programming and implementation of data science, data science theory, and the implications of the business data.

For people to qualify for a data science job, they must possess skills in mathematics, statistics, and a broad knowledge of programming languages such as Python and R. They must also know how to frame a data problem correctly, create questions from it, and report the results correctly.

2. **Data Engineers**

These are the individuals who rely on their expertise in software development to work with large sets of data. They are versatile individuals who use their computer science skills to process large sets of data.

Their focus is on cleaning data sets, coding and implementing any requests that come from data scientists.

Data Engineers have skills in various programming languages including Java and Python. These individuals take a predictive model from a data scientist and translate it into code.

A data engineer should have sufficient knowledge in data storage and warehousing using SQL and NoSQL DBMSs. In addition, he or she must know various programming frameworks like Spark and Hadoop to help source data and process it.

### 3. Data Analysts

These individuals look at the data and provide visualizations and reports to explain the trends and insights hidden in the data. Data Analysts are responsible for helping people understand queries.

Business Analysts are a special kind of Data Analyst who determine the business implications of the data and the actions required.

Should a business invest in project A or project B? The business analyst leverages the work of the data scientists to communicate an answer. Business analysts should have skills in data manipulation using programs such as Excel as well as data communication skills.

Most companies normally hire individuals who will fill up the above roles, so they can benefit from the data they have and the data they will generate in the future.

The individuals filling the various roles normally work together to ensure the organization gets maximum benefit from its data making the task of machine learning easier.

# CONCLUSION

We have come to the end of this guide. The popularity of machine learning is increasing every day, and the field has a very bright future. Machine learning models usually learn from data. The amount of available data doubles every two years. At the same time, the cost of storing this data reduces by the same rate.

In the future, a significant amount of data will be available for use in machine learning. There will also be numerous machine learning tools, and the available ones will have advanced to perform complex machine learning tasks.

Machine learning jobs pay very well. Research has shown it takes longer for companies to hire for machine learning positions compared to other fields.

This is because very few people have majored in the machine learning field. Most machine learning jobs require individuals with advanced degrees.

Clearly, the future of machine learning is bright. Machine learning models can make our work easier and more efficient.

This fact alone should be enough to motivate some of us who are seeking better improvement in our daily routines toward learning machine learning and you are probably one of them.

# Notes

## Chapter 1:

1. https://medium.com/tag/machine-learning
2. http://www.kdnuggets.com/2017/04/top-news-week-0403-0409.html
3. https://yourstory.com/2017/06/techie-tuesdays-anima-anandkumar/
4. https://www.techdirt.com/blog/?tag=machine+learning

## Chapter 2:

1. https://link.springer.com/chapter/10.1007/978-3-662-45489-3_6
2. https://stats.stackexchange.com/questions/145122/real-life-examples-of-markov-decision-processes
3. https://www.ncbi.nlm.nih.gov/pmc/articles/PMC3060044/

## Chapter 3:

1. http://reinforcementlearning.ai-depot.com/
2. http://web.stanford.edu/class/cs234/index.html

3. https://www.analyticsvidhya.com/blog/2017/01/introduction-to-reinforcement-learning-implementation/

4. http://rll.berkeley.edu/deeprlcourse/

5. https://www.quora.com/What-is-reinforcement-learning

## Chapter 4:

1. https://pystruct.github.io/intro.html

2. http://www.nowozin.net/sebastian/cvpr2011tutorial/

3. https://homes.cs.washington.edu/~nasmith/sp4nlp/

4. https://svivek.com/teaching/structured-prediction/spring2017/

## Chapter 5:

1. https://www.analyticsvidhya.com/blog/2017/09/naive-bayes-explained/

2. http://dataaspirant.com/2017/02/06/naive-bayes-classifier-machine-learning/

3. https://monkeylearn.com/blog/practical-explanation-naive-bayes-classifier/

4. https://machinelearningmastery.com/naive-bayes-classifier-scratch-python/

5. http://www.statsoft.com/textbook/naive-bayes-classifier

## Chapter 6:

1. https://www.analyticsvidhya.com/blog/2017/09/understaing-support-vector-machine-example-code/

2. https://docs.opencv.org/2.4/doc/tutorials/ml/introduction_to_svm/introduction_to_svm.html

3. http://scikit-learn.org/stable/modules/svm.html

4. https://machinelearningmastery.com/support-vector-machines-for-machine-learning/

5. https://medium.com/machine-learning-101/chapter-2-svm-support-vector-machine-theory-f0812effc72

6. https://www.kdnuggets.com/2016/07/support-vector-machines-simple-explanation.html

## Chapter 7:

1. https://sebastianraschka.com/blog/2016/model-evaluation-selection-part1.html

2. https://docs.microsoft.com/en-us/azure/machine-learning/studio/evaluate-model-performance

3. https://machinelearningmastery.com/how-to-evaluate-machine-learning-algorithms/

4. http://docs.aws.amazon.com/machine-learning/latest/dg/evaluating_models.html


**Chapter 8:**

1. https://www.datascience.com/blog/common-machine-learning-business-applications

2. https://www.huffingtonpost.com/entry/three-real-use-cases-of-machine-learning-in-business_us_593a0e91e4b014ae8c69df37

3. https://www.techemergence.com/ai-in-business-intelligence-applications/

4. http://www.digitalistmag.com/digital-economy/2017/06/06/machine-learning-rise-of-truly-intelligent-business-applications-05133566

# NOTES

**Chapter 9:**

1. https://www.quora.com/How-exactly-is-machine-learning-used-in-recommendation-engines

2. https://www.analyticsvidhya.com/blog/2016/06/quick-guide-build-recommendation-engine-python/

3. https://www.lynda.com/Python-tutorials/Introduction-Python-Recommendation-Systems-Machine-Learning/563080-2.html

4. https://blog.statsbot.co/recommendation-system-algorithms-ba67f39ac9a3

**Chapter 10:**

1. https://archive.ics.uci.edu/ml/datasets.html

2. http://archive.ics.uci.edu/ml/index.php

3. http://homepages.inf.ed.ac.uk/rbf/IAPR/researchers/MLPAGES/mldat.htm

4. https://www.kaggle.com/uciml/datasets

**Chapter 11:**

1. https://www.ml.cmu.edu/academics/primary-ms.html
2. https://machinelearningmastery.com/16-options-to-get-started-and-make-progress-in-machine-learning-and-data-science/
3. https://www.quora.com/What-are-the-best-graduate-schools-for-studying-machine-learning
4. https://www.admissiontable.com/ms-in-machine-learning/

**Chapter 12:**

1. http://online.stanford.edu/course/machine-learning
2. https://cvn.columbia.edu/program/columbia-university-computer-science-masters-degree-machine-learning-masters-science
3. https://www.class-central.com/subject/machine-learning

4. https://medium.freecodecamp.org/every-single-machine-learning-course-on-the-internet-ranked-by-your-reviews-3c4a7b8026c0

**Chapter 13:**

1. https://blog.udacity.com/2016/04/5-skills-you-need-to-become-a-machine-learning-engineer.html

2. https://www.quora.com/How-should-you-start-a-career-in-Machine-Learning

3. https://www.forbes.com/forbes/welcome/?toURL=https://www.forbes.com/sites/laurencebradford/2017/07/28/8-ways-you-can-succeed-in-a-machine-learning-career/&refURL=https://www.google.com/&referrer=https://www.google.com/

4. https://www.indeed.com/q-Machine-Learning-jobs.html

# Thank You!

Before you go, I would really like to give you a thank you hug for purchasing my book.

You could have picked from the vast selection of other books on the same topic but you took a chance and choose this one.

So, instead of a bear hug, a HUGE thanks to you for getting this book and for being awesome and reading all the way to the end.

It wasn't easy writing this book and my only wish is that more people are able to read my book (great amount of time and efforts have been committed in presenting this book). ***One way you could help is to just take a few minutes to leave an honest review for this book on Amazon.***

This feedback will help me to improve and continues to write the type of books that will help you get the results you are looking for.

Leave your voice here, just click below:

## Machine Learning Series Book #1

Are you clueless about what is machine learning about? Or Are you wondering how can a machine (Deep Blue) beats Garry Kasparov, a reigning world champion in chess?

You are not alone.

Machine learning has been around for more than a decade and yet its usage is still at its infancy.

More companies are investing heavily in machine learning and are reaping generous rewards. Some of these companies products have become an essential part of our daily activities.

*Machine Learning For Beginners: Your Starter Guide For Data Management, Model Training, Neural Networks, Machine Learning Algorithms*

- Learn about the three types of machine learning
- Learn about the machine learning algorithms such as KNN.
- Discover the machine learning tools that you could use
- Learn about data acquisition and data management
- Learn about model training, validation and application
- Learn about how neural networks work and usage.
- Many More..

ISBN 13: 978-1983-4338-63

Go and check out the book at Amazon. Click the link below:

http://strly.cc/krml01

## Machine Learning Series Book #2

Don't you want to learn more about the framework that institutions and companies are using for machine learning? Wouldn't you want to find out the types of real life problems that are solved by various machine learning models?

Machine learning usage has been looming around us yet most of us are still uninformed about its applications and how it can improve their daily life.

KEN RICHARDS

*Machine Learning For Beginners: Your Definitive Guide For Machine Learning Framework, Machine Learning Model, Bayes Theorem, Decision Trees*

- Learn how to choose the machine learning framework in terms of speed, scalability and ease of use.
- Learn how to use the right machine learning model for different types of problems
- More in depth discussion on anomalies and anomaly detection techniques.
- Understand association analysis concepts and rules
- Explore Probability Theory, Bayes Theorem, Decision Trees
- Learn how to optimize your machine learning model
- Many More..

ISBN 13: 978-1983-4339-00

Go and check out the book at Amazon. Click the link below:

http://strly.cc/krml02

Made in the USA
San Bernardino, CA
23 July 2018